Why Does My Shadow Follow Me?

More Science Questions from Real Kids

Written by Kira Vermond   Illustrated by Suharu Ogawa

annick
press

toronto · berkeley

Created in cooperation with the Ontario Science Centre

Cover illustrated by Suharu Ogawa and designed by Paul Covello
Interior designed by Paul Covello
Edited by Claire Caldwell
Copyedited by Becky Noelle
Proofread by Doeun Rivendell
Indexed by Wendy Thomas

Annick Press Ltd.

We acknowledge the support of the Canada Council for the Arts and the Ontario Arts Council, and the participation of the Government of Canada/la participation du gouvernement du Canada for our publishing activities.

Canada

ONTARIO ARTS COUNCIL
CONSEIL DES ARTS DE L'ONTARIO
an Ontario government agency
un organisme du gouvernement de l'Ontario

Library and Archives Canada Cataloguing in Publication

Title: Why does my shadow follow me? : more science questions from real kids / written by Kira Vermond ; illustrated by Suharu Ogawa.
Names: Vermond, Kira, author. | Ogawa, Suharu, 1979- illustrator.
Identifiers: Canadiana (print) 20200327496 | Canadiana (ebook) 2020032750X | ISBN 9781773215013 (hardcover) | ISBN 9781773215037 (HTML) | ISBN 9781773215044 (PDF) | ISBN 9781773215051 (Kindle)
Subjects: LCSH: Science—Miscellanea—Juvenile literature. | LCSH: Technology—Miscellanea—Juvenile literature. | LCSH: Children's questions and answers.
Classification: LCC Q163 .V46 2021 | DDC j500—dc23

Published in the U.S.A. by Annick Press (U.S.) Ltd.
Distributed in Canada by University of Toronto Press.
Distributed in the U.S.A. by Publishers Group West.

Printed in China

annickpress.com
kiravermondkids.com
suharuogawa.com
ontariosciencecentre.ca

Also available as an e-book. Please visit annickpress.com/ebooks for more details.

For Amy B., my rock.
—KV

For Nonoka, Kyusuke, Anne, Ai, Aki, Shisei, Avital, Lior, and Matan.
—SO

Contents

Chapter 4: Tremendous Tech and Inspiring Innovations

Chapter 5: Our Out-of-This-World Universe

Introduction

Congratulations! You're already on your way to becoming a scientist. Yes, that's right. You!

Every time you . . . bake a batch of cookies, squish mud between your fingers,
ride your bike down a hill (yippee!), dunk a basketball through a hoop, or rub a balloon on your
hair and watch it stick to the wall . . . you're running experiments to help yourself explore and
understand the universe around you. "Experiment" is really just another word for play.
And kids are experts at playing!

Real Kids, Real Questions

Every question in this book came from kids who visited the Ontario Science Centre in Toronto, Canada—at a makerspace café called
The Maker Bean, a place where café and technology meet. Here, their amazing and intriguing questions were laser-cut into personalized
wooden coasters to use at the café and start science conversations with other visitors.

Educators and science researchers who work at the Centre came up with the answers for this book. But that's just the beginning! Hopefully
this book will spark some new ideas and get you to ask yourself one very big question: What are you wondering about these days?

Science might have a fancy name or seem complicated, but it really all starts with the process of testing out ideas—again and again—to answer questions.

Take cookie baking. To develop a yummy cookie recipe from scratch, you start with a question. ("What would happen if I added chocolate chips to cookie dough?") If you predict that it will taste good, that's called your "hypothesis." But . . . don't just dive right in! Before mixing and measuring, you'll want to check out other cookie recipes. That way, you'll learn what ingredients work (butter!) or don't (celery!) based on previous bakers' trial-and-error lessons.

Now the fun part! You have to bake many batches, tweaking and testing ingredients as you go to get the best buttery, chocolaty crunch. Then you have to repeat the process—or experiment—numerous times to confirm your results. Tough job, but somebody's got to do it!

Some adults experiment for a living. They actually get paid to play. They're called scientists, and their work touches almost everything around you, from the video games you play to that pizza on your plate. Some of them create medication to save lives or find new ways to heat homes without damaging our beautiful planet. But they don't work alone. Far from it. Scientists all around the world share their questions and answers with each other so everyone can learn together more quickly. And that's where things get really interesting.

Science is sewn into the very fabric of who we are as humans. And all scientific discoveries start with questions just like the ones you'll find in this book. Turn the page and maybe you'll be inspired to ask, test, and repeat, too!

Explore More

Want to get more out of this book? Keep an eye out for cool facts,
insights into scientific breakthroughs—and even experiments for you to try!
Look for titles, "Ask About . . . ," "Play and Learn," and "Share This!"

I've got questions about . . .

Cute Critters
and
Up-ROAR-ious
Creatures

From butterflies that taste with their feet to sea lions that can keep a musical beat, we share the planet with billions of amazing living things. And let's not forget the ancient creatures that roamed and roared millions of years ago. Here's some wild stuff about Earth's most intriguing beings that slink, swim, and soar.

What do cats use their whiskers for?

Those long, stiff hairs on cats' faces aren't just for tickling you. Whiskers—also called "vibrissae"—are highly sensitive tools that help cats navigate the world. You'll find them above the mouth and also above a cat's eyes, and on its ears, its jaw, and the front of its legs! Whiskers even tell you a bit about a kitty's mood. When a cat is relaxed, its muscles relax, too, so the whiskers hang loosely. But when a cat is scared, the muscles pull the whiskers tight against its face.

Whiskers attach to nerve endings deep inside the skin that feed information to the brain. Even a tiny change to a cat's environment will give its whiskers loads of data to process. This super awareness means cats can easily detect prey, find their way in the dark, or even leap onto a narrow ledge without falling off. Speaking of distance, whiskers are usually the same width as a cat's body and can help it figure out if it can s-q-u-e-e-z-e through a small space. Like a built-in measuring tape. The fatter the cat, the wider the whiskers!

Play and Learn

Next time you feed your cat, watch what happens. If your cat scoops food out of her bowl before eating it, she's probably experiencing "whisker stress." Cats don't like it when their whiskers touch anything as they eat. Time to get a bigger bowl.

Why do dogs see in black and white?

They don't. They see colors, too—just not as many as you do. Inside a human eye you'll find cells called "cone cells." They allow us to see color. We have three different kinds. Some are sensitive to red, some green, and others blue. Mixed together, the information collected by our cone cells zips to our brains and we see all the colors of the rainbow. But dogs have only two types of cone cells. They have fewer of them, too. As a result, a dog's world looks less vibrant—yellowish, bluish, and shades of gray.

Don't feel too bad for dogs, though. They have 300 million sensors in their noses (compared to our measly 6 million), so their sniffers are between 10,000 and 100,000 times more powerful than ours. Because dogs experience so much of their world through smell, seeing fewer colors doesn't slow them down.

Paws Off

Never cut a cat's whiskers! That would be like someone taking away your eyesight or sense of touch.

Why don't owls fly in the morning?

Because their meals are on the move at night! Owls are birds of prey. Some eat insects, but others hunt small mammals like mice, shrews, and voles. The largest owls swoop down and grab racoons, possums, and other birds. Many of these yummy animals are nocturnal (active at night), so many owls must hunt at night in order to catch them. Owls have adapted to nighttime hunting by growing massive eyes to see better in the dark and sensitive ears to hear scurrying below. They've also perfected silent flight. And hunting at night means smaller owls are less likely to become meals themselves! By staying hidden during the day, they can avoid predators such as hawks.

But there are exceptions. Owls that spend time in the Far North and the Arctic hunt during the day because they have no choice. In the summertime, daylight lasts and lasts—in some places, the Sun doesn't set for months. If Arctic owls waited for darkness to hunt, they'd starve.

Why do scorpions glow under ultraviolet light?

Scorpions have scary-looking pincers and scaly armor, and some are even deadly poisonous. Not exactly the best pets. But they make great night-lights when sleeping outdoors!

Nearly all scorpions glow brilliant aqua and green as long as there's ultraviolet light (think electric black light or moonlight) shining on them. Scorpions have a hard protective layer outside their bodies called the "exoskeleton"—like a skeleton on the outside of the body. Its coating contains special fluorescent chemicals that absorb ultraviolet light's energy and turn it into an eerie gleam.

Scientists are still puzzled about why scorpions glow. Some believe it helps them find each other in the dark or that it confuses their prey. Maybe there's no point at all! It could just be a random fluke. After all, some rocks glow in ultraviolet light, too. Yet recent experiments show the glow might be like a warning light. It signals to the scorpion that it is not hidden well enough from predators in bright moonlight. Time to seek shelter!

Scorpions for Dinner

The southern grasshopper mouse might look cute and tiny, but if you're a scorpion, watch out! It might just EAT you. These mice not only howl like wolves but will also grab a scorpion, chew off its stinging tail—and dig in. Gulp.

Why don't wasps make honey?

Do you? Of course not. You're not a honeybee. Neither is a wasp.

Although bees and wasps have similarities—they both sting and buzz around backyards, interrupting our picnics—there are many differences between them. Bees love the calorie-dense honey they store in their hives. It's an excellent sugary food source to slurp in cold winter months when flower nectar isn't available. But wasps' lifespans are shorter. They die off when it gets cold. Only one wasp survives: the queen. She hides out in warm underground crevices or building cracks until spring, when she lays her eggs. Even so, many don't make it. Hibernating queen wasps make a tasty treat for spiders!

Wasps might steal honey from a beehive, but they don't make it themselves. Many are omnivores, feeding on small insects or drinking nectar and fruit juices for a quick energy hit.

Heavy Home

In warmer parts of the world, wasp colonies can grow . . . and GROW! One wasp nest found in Tasmania in 2015 weighed a scale-snapping 90 kilograms (198 pounds). That's as heavy as a fully grown male cougar!

Ask About . . . Solitary Wasps

Not all wasps live in colonies. Many species are "solitary wasps," and their eating habits can be pretty gross. Spider wasps sting and paralyze their prey, then give the victim to their babies . . . to eat alive!

Why do bees sting?

Nature has a way of giving creatures amazing tools to defend themselves. Turtles hide inside thick shells for protection. Porcupines grow pointy quills. Bees have defensive weapons, too: their stingers. They sting to protect themselves and the hives they live in. It makes sense. Honeybees spend nearly their entire lives making honey and tending to their baby larvae. Unfortunately for them, wriggly larvae, crunchy eggs, and syrupy honey make a delicious snack for many animals and other insects. Yum!

If bees couldn't protect the hives by stinging these scavengers and predators, all that work would be for nothing.

Honeybees have such a strong drive to defend their hives, they'll even destroy themselves in the process. Strong barbs on the stinger get stuck in the predator's skin. When the bee pulls away, the stinger and part of its tummy remain behind, and the bee dies. The good news? (At least for the bee!) Bees can sting other enemy insects without getting hurt.

What is the oldest animal on Earth?

That depends on what you mean by "oldest animal." Fragile comb jellies and primitive sea sponges were two of the first creatures to evolve on the planet, and they still exist today. They've been around for over 500 million years! And speaking of sea sponges, some species live to be more than 2,000 years old. Scientists think the deep, frigid water causes less damage to their tissues and helps them live that long. But the oldest-underwater-creature award might go to the 5,000-year-old elkhorn coral found in Florida and Caribbean waters—older than the Egyptian pyramids of Giza!

So, what is the world's oldest known land animal right now? His name is Jonathan, and he's a giant tortoise living on the island of St. Helena. Nobody knows for sure how old he is since he was discovered when he was already fully grown, or at least 50 years old. But scientists estimate that the latest Jonathan could have hatched was in 1832. That means he was born nearly 30 years before the first true bicycle was invented!

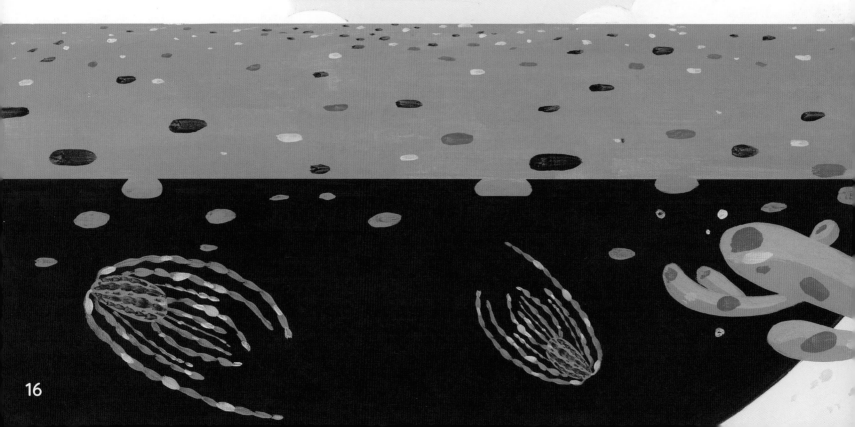

Hungry, Hungry Tortoise

Jonathan might be going blind and deaf in his old age, but he still loves to eat. His favorite foods are lettuce, cabbage, cucumbers, apples, and carrots. He adores bananas, too, but they stick to the roof of his mouth!

Why are sharks so scary?

Umm. Have you seen one of these creatures? Tiger, bull, and great white sharks are huge, powerful swimmers, have razor sharp teeth, and their eyes are not exactly . . . warm. Humans have evolved over millions of years to notice predators, feel fear, and get away fast!

But why do humans seem to dread sharks more than, say, poisonous jellyfish or venomous cone snails? These highly dangerous animals are also found in the ocean. Maybe it's because humans aren't very good at calculating risk. In other words, we see dangers where they don't exist. Or we're unconcerned about real threats. Take vending machines, for example. They don't look very dangerous, do they? But a person is more likely to be hurt by one toppling over than by a shark attack. We should fear vending machines more than sharks, but we don't. And we probably won't until someone makes a movie about enormous killer soda machines!

Ask About . . . Shark Softies

There are over 400 shark species and most are harmless to humans. The dwarf lantern shark is only 20 centimeters (8 inches) long. About the same size as an adult's hand! Meanwhile, the massive whale shark might look ferocious—it is as big as a school bus—but it feeds on tiny shrimp-like plankton, algae, and fish eggs.

Why didn't sharks become extinct with the dinosaurs?

No one knows for sure, but experts have a few ideas. So, let's start with what we do know: sharks are amazing creatures. As a group, they've been around for at least 420 million years, making them much older than dinosaurs and even Mount Everest! By the time the asteroid slammed into Earth 66 million years ago, destroying the dinosaurs and other animals, sharks had already lived through other horrible mass extinction disasters. Including one time when the ocean lost nearly all of its oxygen.

That's not to say the asteroid impact was a picnic for sharks. It hit our planet with the energy of a billion nuclear bombs. The resulting earthquakes were so violent, they shot dinosaurs high into the air. Forests all across North America burned to the ground. Winds swept harsher and faster than any hurricane humans have ever experienced. Dark ash swirled through the atmosphere and blocked the Sun, so many surviving plants eventually died. It's now estimated that at least 70 percent of all animal species went extinct—including many species of sharks.

But a handful survived, along with some fish, frogs, burrowing mammals, birds, turtles, and crocodiles. Scientists think some of the surviving sharks may have dived down deep into the ocean to escape the destruction up above. Sharks are born with the ability to feel vibrations in the water. Did they sense the danger coming and swim down really fast? The disaster may have also created more food for sharks, not less. Tiny creatures at the bottom of their food chain ate decaying plants. Fish ate these critters, and sharks ate the fish. They didn't starve.

Today, sharks are facing a new danger—people. Between overfishing and pollution, many shark species are in trouble. Will they use their same adapting skills to survive us?

Deepwater Shark

The bluntnose sixgill shark has been around for nearly 200 million years—and still swims the cold depths of our oceans today!

Share This!

Some scientists believe early dinosaurs started out as bipeds—walking on two legs. Four-legged dinos evolved later when some developed large stomachs or heavy, spiky armor that needed reinforcement.

How do scientists know a T-Rex was standing on two feet?

When paleontologists uncover bones, they measure the upper arm bone, called the humerus, and the thick thigh bone, the femur. If the arm bones are large and thick compared to the femur, it's likely the dinosaur was quadrupedal and walked on all fours. The strong arms could support its frontal body weight. But a dinosaur like the *Tyrannosaurus rex* had very small arms. There is no way its forelimbs could have supported a heavy chest and massive head full of sharp teeth! This predator didn't stand upright, though. It leaned over and walked parallel to the ground with the help of its heavy tail that acted like a counterweight.

Are birds really dinosaurs?

They really are! The birds we see today evolved from a group of dinosaurs called theropods. That's the same group that *Tyrannosaurus rex* and velociraptors belong to. Many theropods were much smaller, though—and that size likely helped bird-like dinosaurs survive a terrible disaster.

Remember how sharks survived the asteroid that slammed into Earth 66 million years ago (see page 19)? The impact created massive tsunami waves, earthquakes, and raging fires that destroyed forests around the world. Some dinosaur experts now believe all avian (bird) dinosaurs that lived in trees were wiped out in those forest fires. Fortunately, a handful of hardy, ground-dwelling avian dinosaurs were able to find safe places to hide from the heat and fires. Once the coast was clear, they pecked around the gloomy, barren Earth, eating tiny seeds to survive, the experts now think. And of course, their ability to fly meant they could travel without using as much energy as walking. They could swoop away from danger and find food and safer places to live. Over millions of years, these amazing ancient relatives evolved to become the thousands of bird species we know today.

Today's birds still have many of the same features and habits as the ancient theropods, like light, hollow bones; laying eggs and guarding nests; and feathers. (Yes! Some dinosaurs had them, even if they didn't fly.)

We Are Family

Can you guess birds' closest relative today?

A. Bats

B. Flying squirrels

C. Crocodiles

Answer: C (Really! As weird as it seems, birds are technically reptiles. Grrr.)

CHAPTER 2
I've got questions about...
The World Inside Us

Bet you didn't know tongue prints are as unique as fingerprints. Or that your belly button grows tiny hairs to catch belly-button lint (gross!). From your nose to your toes, the human body inspires all kinds of playful, head-scratching questions. Some even tickle the funny bone!

What makes us humans?

Quick! Set this book down and point to all the animals in the room. Did you pick out your friends? Yourself? It's true! You're an animal—a special one called a human. So, what makes you a human rather than a kangaroo, octopus, or screaming hairy armadillo? (They really exist! Look it up.) Short answer? Your deoxyribonucleic acid, also known as DNA.

DNA contains the instructions for building each creature. Human DNA is very similar to a chimpanzee's—we're about 98.8 percent the same. But it's that other 1.2 percent that makes all the difference. Our unique DNA gives us great big brains (at least compared to the rest of our bodies) that help us think deeply and solve problems. We also have a larynx, our voice box, that sits low in our throats so we can speak and make all kinds of different sounds to create language. Our communication skills are top-notch! And don't forget the way we look. Our DNA means we are usually born with ten fingers and toes, stand on two legs, and grow hair on the tops of our heads. DNA is like a recipe for making us who we are!

Why do we have butts?

Love to run? Thank your butt! Human butt cheeks are fat and squishy, but they also house the largest muscle in the entire body: the gluteus maximus. It does the important job of moving the hips and thighs. Every time you climb stairs, bend down, jump rope, or run, this powerhouse muscle goes to work! What's more, it keeps you upright on two legs—a very human trait.

We can see how our butts have changed over time by looking at fossilized skeletons. Muscles leave behind a story in our bones. Some scientists now think strong and efficient gluteus maximus muscles once helped ancient people run for long distances while hunting. They were able to outrun and wear down their prey. Or maybe that strength allowed them to sprint to snatch food that other predators killed! Either way, it seems our brains grew larger around the same time that our hunting abilities improved. Did all of that running, hunting, and problem solving make us smarter? Since big brains set us apart from other animals, it's possible our butts eventually helped make us what we are today: uniquely human!

Why do we grow hair?

Drip. Drip. Drip. Hear that sound? That's your nose without its nose hairs. Every hair on your body—roughly 5 million of them—serves a purpose. For example, those nose hairs keep your slimy, snotty mucus where it's supposed to be: inside your nasal passage. Lashes and brows protect the eyes from dust and keep sweat from trickling into them. And your head's lustrous locks? Some scientists believe the scalp is the hairiest part of the human body because long, thick hair protects the head—the area most exposed to direct sunlight.

That isn't to say humans are otherwise naked. Our bodies are covered in tiny, light vellus hairs. While nearly invisible, this peach fuzz helps wick away sweat and keeps us cool. Each hair is also attached to a sensitive nerve ending. Vellus hair helps you feel the shirt on your back—and that tiny insect creeping along your arm, even if your eyes are closed. Like cats' super-perceptive whiskers, body hair helps you make sense of your world!

How many times can you spin before you puke?

One, two, three . . . whee! The number of times a person can spin before feeling sick—called motion sickness—is different for everyone. Although we do know that kids, women, and people who get migraines are more likely to vomit than others.

Motion sickness happens when your brain experiences a clash between your senses. For example, if you're spinning on a ride at a theme park, your eyes might see the world go by in a wild blur, but your brain is thinking, "Whoa! I'm just sitting here! My muscles aren't doing anything!" Meanwhile, the fluid deep inside your inner ear has a big role to play in motion sickness—especially the moment you put the brakes on. When you spin, the fluid inside spins, too. But if you suddenly stop, that fluid keeps going! While your other senses know you're no longer moving, your inner ears tell your central nervous system a whole different story. The brain can't handle so many mixed signals, so you feel sick until the fluid settles down.

Why does my pee smell?

Pee-yew! What's that smell? If you've been drinking enough water, your pee—also known as urine—shouldn't smell like much of anything. It should also be clear or pale yellow. That's because your body's liquid waste is made of mostly water. But sometimes, things go wrong, and pee gets stinky.

Here's why. When you eat food, your body turns it into energy. This process is called "metabolism." The body takes the nutrients and water it needs by absorbing them into the bloodstream and gets rid of the rest. The leftover liquid waste has to go somewhere. Luckily, most of us have kidneys—two bean-shaped organs that act as blood filters. When blood flows through the kidneys, the organs send water, proteins, and other nutrients back into the bloodstream. What's left? Urine. It then travels to the bladder, where it gets stored until you hit the restroom. If you don't drink enough water and you're dehydrated, urine becomes concentrated—there's too much stinky waste and not enough water—and it will smell strong.

Yuck! Aspara-GAS !

Asparagus contains something called asparagusic acid that makes urine smell unpleasant. But not everyone produces the odor—and some people have "asparagus anosmia." In other words, they can't smell it.

How does sound get to our brains?

What's that? You're curious about how we hear things?

- Let's say your dog barks. Woof! That action creates sound waves—vibrations in the air.

- Those waves travel toward the outer part of your ear, called the "pinna." It's the part you can see, with ridges and folds of cartilage and skin.

- The sound waves continue their journey into the ear canal, which is covered in sticky earwax and tiny hairs that collect dirt and prevent infections.

- The end of the canal leads to a paper-thin membrane called the eardrum. It passes the vibrations on to three tiny bones. One of them—the U-shaped stapes—is the tiniest bone in your body! These bones make the vibrations stronger.

- Vibrations transfer to the inner ear, your cochlea. It's spiral shaped, like a snail, and full of sloshy fluid and thousands of tiny hair cells. These cells turn vibrations into electrical signals that move through your auditory nerve to the brainstem, then onto the final destination, your auditory cortex. This is where your brain decodes these electrical signals so you can hear your pooch bark!

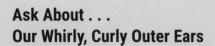

Ask About . . .
Our Whirly, Curly Outer Ears

Why do our outer ears have so many twists and folds? They've evolved to be especially good at picking up the sound of the human voice.

Do we all see color the same?

We have no idea! Two people can spend all day describing a stunning sunset's hues and shades, but neither can see through the other's eyes. That's not to say one person's yellow is another person's purple. Most people have three color-sensitive receptors in the backs of their eyes. So, if you see a can of blue paint, your brain thinks, "My brain is getting an impression about that paint. Everyone else is calling it blue, so I'll call it blue." But . . . what are you actually seeing? Navy blue, teal blue, sky blue, or robin's egg blue? What is blue for you?

Some people have fewer than three color receptors and can't recognize all tints and tones. We call this color blindness. Others have a fourth receptor and see extra colors the rest of us don't. It's a very rare condition, but imagine how much fun art class would be if you had it!

滝団地北

Red Light, Blue Light!

Your culture can influence how you experience color. For a long time in Japan, there was no word for green. It was considered a shade of blue, or 青 (ao). Today, traffic lights that tell cars to go are still called "blue" in Japan!

Why are games so fun?

Because they make us happy and help us learn new things! Take a simple game like peekaboo. Babies love to play it because it helps them figure out the world. When grown-ups cover their faces, babies might be thinking, "Where did they go?" It's a puzzle, and our brains really love puzzles! The baby becomes a mini scientist trying to figure out what happens next. Will the grown-up come back and yell "peekaboo" every time? Only sometimes? Is there a pattern? The same idea goes for more complex games like soccer, Monopoly, or a favorite video game. We enjoy them because they give our brains what they crave:

- social time with friends and family

- goals to accomplish so we can compete (and win!)

- rules and more rules

Finally, games help us relax, which is a great thing because that's how we learn best.

Play and Learn

♣ Even crocodiles love to frolic and play! Some have been known to toss a ball around and give their friends piggyback rides.

33

Will humans ever fly?

We already have. In airplanes, helicopters, and gliders—
just not using our own bodies powered by our own muscles.

Here's why it will likely never happen: Our amazing bodies have evolved
over millions of years so we can run, jump, and play. But compared to birds
and most other airborne creatures, our muscles are too small, inefficient, and
weak to be much good for flying—even if we had wings. Our bones are also
heavy, unlike bird bones, which are light and hollow. And forget skin and hair.
They definitely don't help with flapping and flying! But feathers do.

That's not all. Humans are simply not aerodynamic enough for flight—our bodies
are too wide and flat. When air hits us, our bodies create a force called "drag."
Drag makes it harder to move through air (and water).
Birds' bodies are elongated and curved, so they push through air easily.

Just think about a bird's face
compared to yours!

pointed head

round face

beak

jaw

See? Best to leave flying to the birds
(and qualified airplane pilots).

Time for Takeoff!

Forget flying squirrels. (Despite their name,
they glide.) Bats are the only mammals
capable of true flight. Like birds, they have
powerful chests. Their bones are also slim
and light. But bats' wide wings are made
of a thin membrane, much like the webbing
between your toes, instead of feathers.

Is genetic mutation that creates super abilities possible?

Not only is it possible, it happens all the time!
But maybe not in the way you would expect.

The genes in our bodies' tiny cells carry important information about our traits and what we look like: brown versus green eyes, big or little feet, and even whether we snort when we laugh! Many of these traits are passed down through families. But sometimes, genes don't work right. They either start out different from the time we are born, or change over time. When genes change, it's called "mutation." Some mutations can cause medical problems like color blindness, blood diseases, and even cancer.

But sometimes mutated genes can create amazing and helpful "superpowers"! There's the "sports gene," called *ACTN3*, which controls muscles and can make athletes super strong and fast. People with the *hDEC2* "short sleeper" mutation can wake up feeling rested and chipper after getting only four hours of sleep. There's even a mutation that makes bones extremely dense and practically unbreakable. How did scientists discover this genetic superpower in one American family? A young person walked away from a serious car collision without a single broken bone!

Our genetic mutations may never give us the ability to leap over tall buildings, blast lightning from our fingertips, or fly, but little mistakes in our genes still lead to some incredible human skills, talents, and powers.

Cell Power

Your body is made of billions of cells, and each cell contains about 25,000 to 35,000 genes.

CHAPTER 3
I've got questions about…

This Planet We Call Home

Sure, we might be the third planet from the Sun, but Earth is number one when it comes to sharing the things we need to live and thrive: liquid water to drink, fresh air to breathe, fertile land to farm—and even an atmosphere to protect us from space! Check out these questions about our beloved 4.5-billion-year-old home.

Why do we have to go outside?

Because it makes us happier! All kinds of scientific studies show that spending time outdoors makes us less stressed and physically healthier. Research has shown that when cities plant more trees and swap concrete for grass, crime rates even go down! People venture outside more and get to know their neighbors when there is greenery outside.

Some researchers believe humans are wired to be outside because our brains crave novelty. We like things that are different. So, while the insides of our homes don't change very much, every time we head outdoors, we sense the wind blowing, hear insects buzzing, see leaves rustling, and smell the mud underneath our feet. Our brains pick up all these exciting changes, and our bodies respond.

Exposing ourselves to the Sun also helps set our bodies' circadian rhythm—the internal clock that helps with sleep and digestion. We need the Sun to keep that clock running properly.

Play and Learn

Go ahead, put down this book and play outside. Take a hike, meet your friends at the park, explore your neighborhood, or plant some seeds in your backyard or on your balcony. Even looking outside at greenery from your window can cause your heart rate to go down. You'll feel calmer. Try it! Your brain and body will thank you!

How did water get on Earth?

By hitching a ride on asteroids! At least that's what many scientists suspect.

When Earth was still a young planet billions of years ago, it was likely bombarded by debris, our solar system's space gravel. The comets that hit the Earth contained water ice. Astronomers once thought that the oceans were first created when this ice melted.

Or maybe not. Recent tests have shown that comet water isn't very similar to Earth water, so they couldn't have been the planet's main source of H_2O. But water found on asteroids? It's a much better match. Another theory suggests our water was made even closer to home: in our solar nebula, the massive cloud of dust and ash remaining after our Sun formed. It might also explain why we have so much water on our planet. Either way, it's a good thing Earth is in what we call the "Goldilocks Zone." At 150 million kilometers (93 million miles) from the Sun, we're not so hot that Earth's water boils and turns to steam, nor so cold that it freezes all at once. The temperature is just right for making the oceans, lakes, and rivers we love to splash around in!

What makes volcanoes explode?

Frothy, bubbly, blazingly hot magma! This molten rock is created deep inside the Earth. When the large, thin rock plates that cover our planet's surface spread apart, slip side by side, or even scrape over each other, this movement creates enough heat and energy to literally melt rock below!

Magma is lighter than regular rock, though, so it pushes toward the Earth's surface. As it rises, tiny gassy bubbles form. If the magma is thin like apple juice, the bubbles have no trouble escaping into the air. Eventually the hot magma reaches the surface and oozes through vents in the Earth's crust to create slow-moving lava flows. But if the magma is thick and sticky like honey, the bubbles get stuck. The magma can block off vents, too. Pressure builds and builds . . . until the crust explodes! The force can shoot giant boulders almost a kilometer (0.62 miles) away!

Specialists called volcanologists study volcanoes' histories to determine how often they blow. They then use special equipment to predict eruptions. It's not an exact science, though. While data might show pressure building beneath the Earth's surface, it's hard to know precisely when the release will come and how destructive it will be. Luckily, there have been amazing success stories. Nearly 20,000 people were evacuated from the danger zone at the base of Mount St. Helens in Washington before it erupted in 1980.

Share This!

Although volcanoes can be very destructive, they do a lot of good, too. In fact, we have volcanoes to thank for creating much of the ground we stand on. Ancient volcanic rock makes up at least a third of every continent! Today's volcanic eruptions continue to create islands, mountains, and fertile soil for farming. Scientists are even coming together to study ways to tap volcanoes' thermal energy to power homes.

Ask About . . . Magma and Lava

When it flows below the Earth's surface, hot liquid rock is called "magma." When it's aboveground, we call it "lava."

Why are flowers different colors?

Flowers are pretty, but they also have a purpose: to spread their pollen and make more plants. The best way to do that? Look attractive to birds or insects so they'll land on the flowers and fly away covered in powdery pollen. In some cases, flowers try to tempt specific birds or insects. For instance, some red flowers attract birds but not bees. Butterflies can't get enough of bright red, yellow, and orange flowers. How about flowers that try to lure garbage-loving flies? These species have actually evolved to look and smell like rotting meat: dark red or purple, and stinky.

Not all flowers are pollinated by little creatures. Wind-pollinated flowers don't have to put on a show to attract anybody. But don't let their soft colors fool you into thinking they're dull. Because their pollen is light enough to be carried by the breeze, we breathe it in. Hello, allergies. Achoo!

Why is a cactus prickly?

All living things need water, including cacti. But the environments where cacti typically live are hot and dry. Plants grow s-l-o-w-l-y in harsh places. If a mammal, insect, or other creature munched on a desert cactus, it would take a long time for that plant to grow back to its pre-snack size. Cacti grow spines for protection. Would you like to eat a mouthful of prickles? Of course not! And neither would animals that live in the desert.

Some spines also collect dew. Any moisture in the air forms a tiny droplet of water on a spine's tip and then trickles toward the stem. And although spiny spikes don't look lush to us, they still create shade for the plant. The shade keeps the cactus cool and protects it from the Sun—much like how the hair on your head protects your scalp from the Sun. Who knew you had something in common with a cactus?

How do mirrors reflect?

Look at your hand. It's reflecting enough light so your eyes can see it. In fact, everything on the planet reflects some amount of light. Including mirrors! And that's why you're able to gaze upon your reflection in the restroom mirror (ooh la la!). But unlike your hand, which is covered in tiny bumps, mirrors are made of incredibly smooth glass with a thin layer of silvery metal on the back. Without any texture, the mirror reflects nearly all the light on your face and bounces it back toward your eye at the exact same angle as before. You see these perfectly reflected beams of light as a mirror image.

What color is sunlight?

Yellow? Nope. It's white! Sunlight is made up of all the colors our eyes can see: red, orange, yellow, green, blue, indigo, and violet. But when they come together, our brains tell us they're white.

Play and Learn

Ever hang a glass suncatcher prism in the window? When the Sun's white light hits it at a certain angle, the prism breaks it up into those seven colors and turns them into a twirling rainbow on the wall or floor. That's because different colors of light travel at different speeds. When white light enters the prism, the prism changes the speed, so each color exits at a different angle instead of coming out as one beam of white light. Water droplets can act as prisms, too, which is why you'll sometimes see a rainbow when the Sun comes out right after a rainstorm.

Why does my shadow follow me?

You know when your toe gets stuck through a hole in your sock? That hole isn't a thing. It's simply a space where material used to be. Shadows are like that, too. Shadows are spots that are missing light from the Sun or a light bulb. So, when you look on the ground and see your shadow, you're actually looking at light falling on the ground around you except for the area where your body blocks it. Your shadow follows your every move because your own body is creating shade. When you move, so does your shady shadow.

Proton   Neutron   Electron

How does static make hair fly?

Have you ever rubbed a balloon against your hair and stuck it to the wall? Been zapped by an electric shock? Seen a bolt of lightning streak across the sky? That's static electricity!

To understand static, it's important to know everything on the planet is made of tiny particles called atoms. Inside these atoms are even smaller subparticles called protons, neutrons, and electrons. Protons and neutrons are usually at the center of an atom and love to hang out together. But electrons are on the move, zipping around them. Each subparticle also carries a little bit of electric charge. Protons have a positive charge, neutrons have a neutral charge, and electrons have a negative charge.

Here's the interesting thing about electrons: they can jump to another atom! Say you take your winter hat off. As you remove your hat, electrons move from your hair to the hat. Suddenly you have more negative electrons on the hat and leftover positive protons on your hair. We say the hat has a "negative charge" and your hair has a "positive charge." When it comes to subparticles, opposites attract. Two materials with different charges (a positive and negative) pull toward each other. But if you have two negative charges or two positive charges, they push each other away.

After taking off your hat, your hair strands are all positively charged, so they lift, fan out, and try to get away from each other. Talk about a hair-raising experience!

Play and Learn

The silver static electricity ball you see at science museums is called a Van de Graaff generator. To make it work, a nylon or rubber belt inside spins close to a metal comb—and steals electrons from it, giving the comb and attached ball a positive charge. When you touch the silver ball, it wants to get its electrons back, so it steals them from you! But because you're standing on a special surface called an "insulator," you can't steal more electrons from the ground beneath you. Every part of you now has a positive charge, including your hair and scalp. When you shake your head, your hair will lift straight up and stand on end in a halo of staticky strands!

How many people live on Earth?

About 8 billion. Although depending on when you read this, there will likely be hundreds of millions more. That's great news! With better medicine and education, more adults and kids around the world are living longer, healthier lives. But isn't there also a downside to this never-ending population growth? Maybe you worry it will put a massive strain on our planet's resources. There will be less land for farming and water for drinking.

A lot of people are worried about that. But here's more good news. Population experts now agree the numbers will level off.

In 2018, for the first time in history, people aged 65 outnumbered little kids worldwide. The numbers have been increasing partly because people are living longer. The world is also becoming a better place to live in overall. More people have more money, education, and access to healthcare than ever before. And research has shown that the more of these improvements a family experiences, the fewer children they have. As the older generation begins to die away, and with fewer babies to replace them, the Earth's population will stop growing.

CHAPTER 4

I've got questions about . . .

Tremendous Tech and Inspiring Innovations

Technology is about more than gizmos and gadgets to play with. Using scientific knowledge, technology develops creative ways to make life better, safer, and more fun! Imagine a world without phones, antibiotics, or school buses! (Okay, maybe not school buses.) The following questions are cutting-edge.

How do you get the strawberry in the strawberry candy?

You don't. There's usually no strawberry in strawberry candy at all. But candy makers are very good at adding strawberry flavor to their sweets.

Flavors, which are all made up of both scent and taste, are small chemical mixtures, or "compounds." The flavor that we think of as strawberry is actually a combination of several compounds that make that juicy berry taste (and smell). When a candy company wants to add flavor to their jawbreakers, gum, or jelly beans, special chemists called flavorists take strawberry puree and extract the molecules that make the taste. Or they develop brand-new molecules that look exactly the same as those found in strawberries! There can be a lot of trial and error to get the taste just right.

So, go ahead and pop a strawberry candy in your mouth. Just don't use its technical flavor name—ethyl methylphenylglycidate—unless you want to confuse people!

Why does my bag of popcorn explode after microwaving for two minutes?

Thank water for that. Popcorn kernels come from a special kind of corn with a very hard outer shell. Inside? You'll find starch and water. When you turn on your microwave oven, it gives energy in the form of microwaves to whatever is inside. The microwaves cause the tiny water molecules inside to vibrate, creating a lot of heat. When the trapped water inside each kernel turns into super-heated steam, pressure builds and pushes against the kernel's tough shell. Eventually, the pressure becomes too much, and just like a balloon—POP! The shell explodes, and the soft starch spills out and cools into a fluffy shape. Voilà! Popcorn.

A similar process happens to the microwave bag. The steam from the popping kernels gets trapped in the closed bag, building pressure until it bursts, letting that steam out.

Ask About . . . Steam Energy

Stand back! Popcorn kernels can pop almost a meter (3 feet) into the air.

53

Why is glue sticky?

There are all kinds of adhesives in the world: beeswax, strawberry jam, tar, and even a synthetic one that copies the tiny hairs on gecko feet. Amazing! There's also the everyday white glue you probably use at school. It's made of polymers, groups of tiny molecules that link together in long chains. These polymers are adhesive (sticky) and cohesive (they stick to themselves). They're also strong and elastic. Adding water to polymers makes glue more spreadable, but when it meets air, the water evaporates and changes from a liquid to a gas. Without water, the adhesive dries out and hardens. This causes the molecules to stick together even more. Luckily, it takes a while for the water in white glue to evaporate, which is why it's not easy to glue your fingers together in art class—unless you have a lot of time (and glue) on your hands.

How does an X-ray see through bodies?

Ouch! You just broke your arm! Time to head to the hospital and get an X-ray. But don't worry. It's not going to hurt. An X-ray is simply a form of light that humans are unable to see. Although, some special cameras can. You know how dogs tilt their heads when they hear a really high whistle—even though you don't pick up the note? That doesn't mean the sound doesn't exist. It's just that humans can't hear it. The same goes for X-ray light.

To picture how an X-ray works, face a window, close your eyes, and then wave your hand in front of your face. You saw your hand's shadow, right? Light went right through your eyelids to make the image! Although we don't think of our skin as being translucent, it does let some light through. So do our muscles. X-rays travel easily through this tissue. But not so for hard, dense bone. When X-ray light shines through the body, and the special camera captures the image, bone appears as a ghostly shadow.

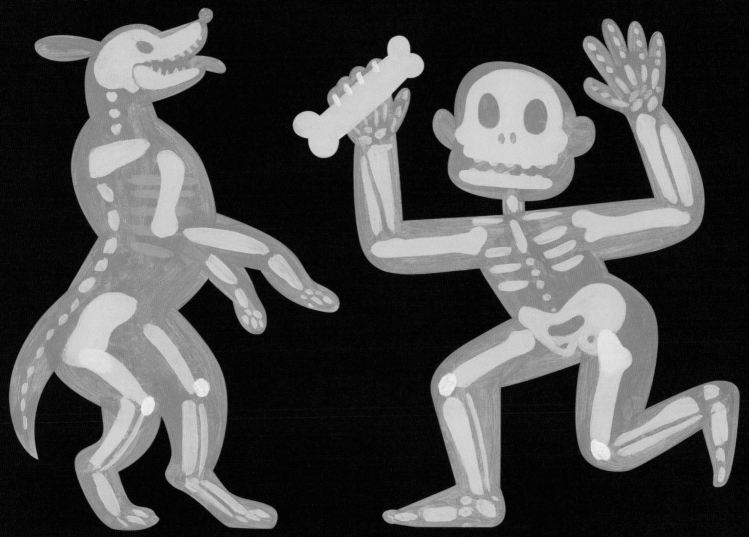

When will they cure cancer?

Which kind do you mean? Cancer is actually a family of diseases. There are over 100 different types and there's no single cure for all of them.

Cancers grow when normal cells mutate and change. Cells usually detect this damage and fix themselves. Or they even self-destruct. But sometimes, that doesn't happen. Some cells go rogue! Instead of aging and dying, these mutated cells keep growing and dividing until they invade tissue. There are many reasons why cells are unable to fix themselves. Sometimes people are exposed to chemicals or too much sunlight, or they get an infection that can lead to cancer under the right conditions. Or maybe they were born with a family cancer gene. Approaching how we treat disease can depend on how people get it in the first place. It's complicated.

Luckily, scientists and doctors are always testing new treatments, medicine, and technologies that save more lives every year.

Share This!

Some researchers are developing new vaccines that are expected to keep people safe from ever getting some types of cancer at all. Many children already receive one of these vaccines today. We're also finding ways to catch cancer early before it grows and spreads. We are making progress all the time. Maybe someday *you* will find a way to cure a type of cancer!

Can stem cells bring back the dead?

Our bodies are made up of many types of cells that have specific jobs. Red blood cells move oxygen through our bloodstream. Other cells create our skin and hair. Liver cells are, well, liver cells. But stem cells are unique. They have the ability to change into many different cell types. Need to repair heart muscle or brain tissue? Make new skin for people who have been badly burned? Offer a dose of healthy blood cells to sick cancer patients using their own blood? Stem cells are on the case! (With a lot of help from scientists and doctors.) The scientific field is exploding with possibilities.

So, can we use these amazing cells to bring the dead back to life? A spooky thought, isn't it? Imagine a walking horde of stem-cell-activated zombies!

But no. Scientists have never been able to use these special cells in this way. The procedure is too complicated. It also brings up some tough ethical questions: What would the person's life be like after she comes back from the dead? What medical consequences might be awaiting her down the road? So far, no one knows the answers, and researchers aren't willing to take the chance.

Can we live forever one day?

Medical science has given us new drugs and surgery methods that keep us living longer than ever before. In fact, in 1960, the average person in North America lived to be 70 years old. Today, it's closer to 79. But longer life brings new challenges. Older adults are more likely to get diabetes and cancer. Or their brains and hearts stop working as well as they used to. Our bodies seem to have a time limit, no matter what we do.

That isn't to say we aren't still trying to find ways to beat the clock. Scientists are looking into mind immortality—uploading a mind into a computer—so when the body dies, the mind lives on. Other experts are experimenting on mice to see if they can reverse aging in humans' cells someday.

But even if we could live forever, would we want to?

What would happen to the planet if no one ever died?

What would a 500-year-old person look like, anyway?

Would you want to live inside a computer for eternity?

What do *you* think?

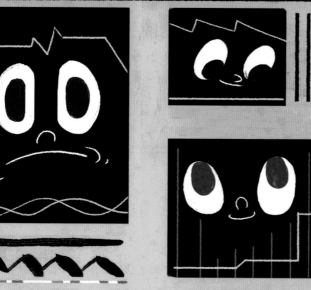

Why do we pollute?

Humans are creative, intelligent, and inventive. From the time we built the first wheel, we've been figuring out ways to make our lives better and easier. Think about all the inventions that help you every day! Someone had to design your backpack that makes walking to school less tiring. Your food doesn't rot because you've got a chilly refrigerator and plastic wrap that keep it fresh longer. And chances are, your house is warm in the winter because you have a furnace or electricity for heat.

But all of these amazing inventions come at a cost. Sometimes they have unintended consequences and create new problems— like pollution. We need energy to warm and cool our homes and to drive our cars and buses. Often, that energy comes from burning the fossil fuels we dig from the ground. Burning them releases gases and tiny particles into the air that make it harder to breathe and can even change our climate! Meanwhile, there's the pollution we can see with our own eyes. Our trash ends up littering our land and water.

The good news? More people around the world now understand that although there are many benefits to an easier life, it's also important to find ways to keep Earth healthy. While scientists and engineers are inventing ways to harness green energy sources and build low-emission cars, kids just like you are making a difference, too. From using microbes to speed up plastic bag decomposition to designing temporary housing from recycled materials for natural disaster victims, there are all kinds of innovative ways to reduce, reuse, and recycle the products and energy that make our lives easier. No one puts "pollute" on their to-do list, but we can all dream up new ways to put an end to pollution and take action.

Play and Learn

Heading out for a hike or for a day at the beach? Bring an empty bag with you and pick up any trash along the way. What do you find? Is there a way to reuse it and turn it into something amazing?

How does information travel so fast on the Internet?

Computers just can't get enough of these two numbers: 0 and 1. Almost everything—music, messages, pictures, and movies—can be represented as a string of zeros and ones in binary code, or computer language. Computers turn those numbers into pulses of dim and bright light and send them through glass fiber cables that spread all over the planet. Think of this network as small spiderwebs connecting office buildings or neighborhoods within giant webs lying at the bottom of oceans linking continents. The Internet is a network of networks.

Remember those light pulses? Light travels fast. Really fast. As in 1,079,252,848 kilometers per hour (670,616,629 miles per hour) fast. Glass slows it down a little, but even so, when light travels inside these glass fibers, the pulses can zip around planet Earth five times every second! Once they reach your house, the light pulses turn into radio waves—or Wi-Fi—another form of speedy light energy sent through the air. Enjoy your movie!

Share This!

Antarctica is the only continent that does not have glass fiber cables running to it. Scientists and engineers combined their efforts to give people who work and live there Internet service through satellite.

Is there Wi-Fi in space?

Have you ever seen a loooong cable running between the International Space Station and Earth? Of course not. Astronauts communicate with NASA and their families using wireless technology. They even have movie nights and stream films! NASA has actually created three different types of networks to make wireless communication possible. The Space Network connects satellites, the Near Earth Network connects space missions, and the Deep Space Network reaches far into the solar system. Wi-Fi—radio signals that connect satellites, spacecraft, and astronauts back to planet Earth—isn't perfect though. Right now, if you wanted to send a message to a person living on Mars, there would be a 20-minute delay, even though the signals are traveling near the speed of light!

CHAPTER 5
I've got questions about ...

Our Out-of-This-World Universe

Think you might want to be an astronaut someday? Love to spread out at night and look up into the twinkling heavens? No matter where an interest in space takes you, these stellar questions might leave you starstruck.

Play and Learn

Look up. Beautiful green, yellow, and red auroras are actually oxygen atoms interacting with Sun particles. Nitrogen makes dancing blue and purplish-red lights.

Why do northern lights exist?

Northern lights (aurora borealis) and southern lights (aurora australis) are magical displays of shimmering, dancing, colorful lights in the night sky. If you live near the North or South Poles, maybe you have even seen them! To create the show, you need four ingredients: Earth's magnetic field, charged particles from the Sun, solar wind, and gases in our atmosphere.

The Earth's strong magnetic field begins deep in the planet's core and extends way out into space. Sometimes the Sun blasts HUGE explosions of charged particles, and gusts of solar winds spiraling outward carry them throughout the solar system. When these winds blow past Earth, our magnetic field grabs some particles and pulls them toward the North and South Poles where the field is strongest. As these particles rain down on Earth, they excite gases like oxygen and nitrogen in our atmosphere. Suddenly—poof! There's a burst of colored light! These auroras are our

Why is there no gravity in space?

Forget the term "zero gravity." It's confusing. In reality, there is gravity in space, but it's very, very low. We call this state "microgravity." And it's a good thing it exists. Imagine what would happen if there was no gravity in the cosmos at all. Astronauts walking on the Moon would float up and never come down! Even worse, planets would no longer circle the Sun. The Moon would stop orbiting the Earth. They would all drift away from each other forever. The solar system as we know it would disappear. Gravity—the invisible force that pulls objects toward each other—keeps everything in place.

Attractive Hero

Our magnetic field is very important. Without it, we would be exposed to harmful radiation from the Sun and most of our atmosphere would escape into space

Ask About . . .
Gravity on Earth

Coming back to Earth after weeks in microgravity can be tough on the body and mind. One astronaut revealed he once forgot he was no longer in space and let go of a bottle of aftershave in midair. Of course, it smashed on the floor!

When will the Sun explode?

It won't. Only larger stars with many times the mass of our Sun can experience a supernova explosion—the powerful and bright blast at the end of a star's life cycle. Instead, our Sun will eventually get heavier and bigger as it runs out of hydrogen gas, and heavier elements like oxygen and carbon form.

When hydrogen atoms collide inside the Sun, it creates an incredible amount of heat and pressure that fuses the hydrogen together—also known as "nuclear fusion." Eventually, the Sun will start to run out of regular hydrogen and become less stable. At this stage it will grow bigger than any of us can imagine. Our Sun will be so large it will hit Earth's orbit! For millions of years it will glow bright red and swell into a "red giant" star, expelling its outer gases into space. Eventually, only the core of the dead star, also known as a "white dwarf," will be left behind.

But our Sun has a lot of life left in it. Astronomers believe our Sun has enough hydrogen to keep going strong for another 5.4 billion years. Whew!

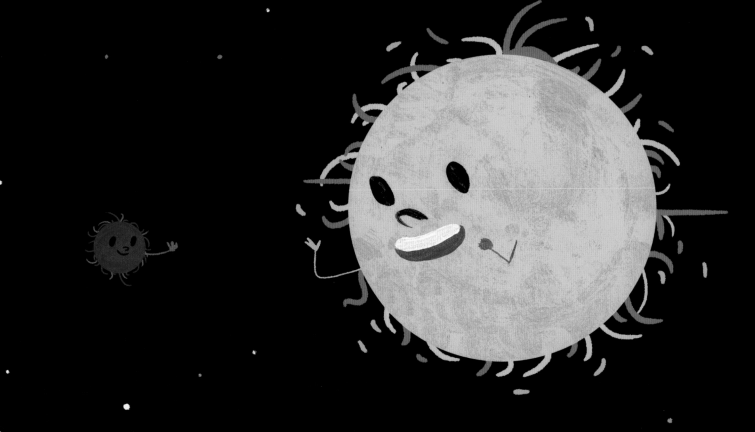

What is the coldest star?

Say hello to "red dwarf" stars, the coldest in the universe. These common stars are much smaller than our Sun and not as bright. Because they're smaller and have less fuel, they burn at a lower temperature—about 3,500 degrees Celsius (6,332 degrees Fahrenheit). That's about half as hot as our Sun's surface, which is a sizzling 5,500 degrees Celsius (9,932 degrees Fahrenheit).

Share This!

What's a star that isn't really a star? Within the last decade, astronomers have discovered a handful of "brown dwarf" stars that are as warm as a cup of coffee or cold as the North Pole! Unlike the blazing-hot stars we normally think of, brown dwarfs fuse deuterium (heavy hydrogen) and lithium instead of fusing hydrogen in their core. So, are they really stars? Some say they rest in a confusing place between star and planet and may someday earn a whole new category altogether.

Does bacteria grow in space?

Yes, and it's a good thing, too. Without bacteria, astronauts wouldn't survive. As humans, we actually have 10 times as many bacterial cells as human cells inside us and on our skin. (Although bacterial cells are smaller and weigh less—about 1.4 kilograms [3 pounds] in total—roughly the weight of your brain.) Bacteria helps us digest our food, keeps us safe from infection, and repairs damaged tissue. Bacteria is so important to our health, scientists blasted it into space before humans. When they saw that bacteria survived the journey, the experts saw it as a good sign for people! Today, astronauts conduct experiments with bacteria in space, and some bacteria even live on the outside of the International Space Station without oxygen.

So far, though, the only bacteria we've found in space is our own.

Why are there astronauts in space when we have robots?

Because it's a good idea to have both. Space exploration robots are very rugged and strong. We can shoot them into the solar system without worrying about their health and safety, particularly when encountering extreme temperatures and radiation. They can also travel for years and even decades without needing food, sleep, or trips to the bathroom. But humans have something special going for us. We're able to think quickly on our feet and solve problems without anyone needing to program us like a computer.

A rover robot can go to Mars, take beautiful images, pick up a rock, and drill down into an alien planet's surface, but we need humans to describe what they see, hear, taste, smell, and touch there. We explore the cosmos because we're curious. That inquisitive human heart and mind belong in space, too.

Share This!

Scott Parazynski, a medical doctor who was on the International Space Station a few years back, used his surgery skills to repair a hole in a broken solar panel. His human creativity saved the day!

How far is it possible to go in a spaceship?

Theoretically, we could travel anywhere in the universe, even billions of light-years away, although it would be far from easy and take a very long time. At this point, humans have gone only as far as the Moon, 385,000 kilometers (239,228 miles) away. But that will change when the next generation of rockets launches the *Orion* spacecraft to take astronauts to Mars—a nine-month trip! Think that's far? Space is so vast that if we rocketed to the next known star, Proxima Centauri, it would take generations to get there. Maybe your grandchildren's grandchildren will get a chance to see it!

We've had better luck sending uncrewed spacecraft far into space. *Voyager 1* blasted off in 1977 and is now about 150 times farther away from the Sun than we are. This spacecraft left our solar system behind in 2012. And it's still going!

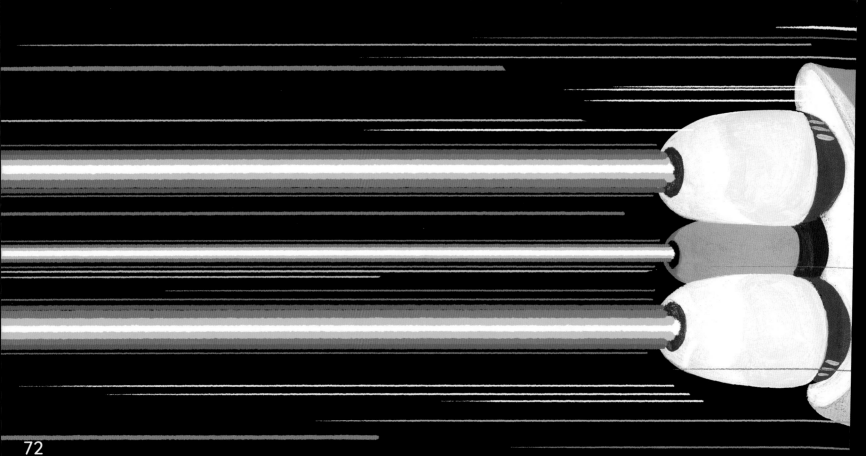

How do people survive on Mars?

We don't know. But that's because no human has ever been there. At least, not yet.

People definitely want to travel to our solar system's "Red Planet" though. Decades of scientific research and exploration are already paving the way to make it happen. For instance, we've learned how to grow lettuce in microgravity on the International Space Station. Astronauts wipe the leaves with little brushes because there aren't any bees on board to pollinate the plants. With this knowledge, travelers to Mars might grow fresh food there someday. That would be an incredible achievement!

We don't have to run all of our experiments in space, either. We can do some right here on Earth. Mars gets painfully cold, so we have built Mars simulators in the frigid Arctic and Antarctic. Scientists are also training astronauts inside lava tubes in Spain. These underground labs imitate what it would be like to live deep below the surface of Mars to escape harmful radiation.

Even if we find ways to live in extreme environments, there are still other difficult engineering obstacles to overcome. With no gas stations along the six- to nine-month journey to Mars, the spaceship would have to carry all of its own fuel. And how would we find water once we arrived there?

Alone in the Universe

Remember how restless you felt at home during the early days of the COVID-19 pandemic? You probably wanted to go outside, play, and see your friends. Now imagine being sealed inside a small metal space cylinder for six to nine months— the time it takes to reach Mars! Isolation experiments show that not everyone is cut out to make such a long journey so far from home. How about you?

But perhaps the biggest challenge would not be found on the planet, but inside our own bodies. The longer people live in low Mars gravity, the worse it would be for their bones and muscles. Unless scientists find a way to deal with this pressing medical issue, astronauts could be too weak and frail to return to Earth.

Fortunately, research into strengthening bodies and even making fake gravity is already underway. With our creativity, imagination— and by working together—humans can achieve amazing scientific feats!

Play and Learn

Go ahead. Stand on a bathroom scale on Mars. What do you weigh? Because Mars is small and has less mass than Earth, its gravitational pull is about three-eighths of our own. So if you weighed 40 kilograms (88 pounds) on Earth, you would tip the scales at 15 kilograms (33 pounds) as a martian. What would you weigh on Mars? Do the math!

Conclusion

From the fiery magma flowing beneath your feet to the twinkling spray of stars above, the universe inspires so many amazing questions! And there are still millions of questions to research and explore. In fact, the 50 questions in this book are only a tiny fraction of the ones that kids like you asked us. But including answers to all of them would have made this book way too heavy for your backpack!

Questions like . . .

How do cats purr?

When will we have technology for flying cars?

Why do we need air?

How does using a toilet work in space?

And even . . .

How long does it take a snake to digest a chicken? (Easy answer: not quickly enough! Eww.)

See? Our brains are full of questions we ask to make sense of our world. But in order to find answers and gain more knowledge, we run experiments and test ideas. We play! That sometimes means figuring things out as we go along—and making loads of mistakes along the way.

But that's okay. Every wrong turn means learning something new to pass on to other people. Just consider all the answers in this book. In most cases, to find them, there was no one scientist yelling "Eureka!" alone in a lab. Instead, there were dozens or even hundreds of people all around the world developing theories, testing results for years—and getting them wrong again and again. Mistakes help us gain valuable information together. And with that kind of teamwork, there's no stopping humans and our craving for knowledge.

Which brings us to one final question asked by a kid just like you:

Is the sky really the limit?

Yes and no. A starry sky is certainly as far as our human eyes can see. It's the visual limit of our physical world. But thousands of years of science, art, creativity, and human effort to explore the heavens have given us telescopes, satellite images, and brave astronauts in space. Our curiosity has given human beings a new perspective about our place in the universe. Once we blasted off Earth, sliced through the sky, walked on the Moon, and floated with planets and stars, limits seemed to fade away.

The sky is still there, but we now see further. Dream further. And someday we will go further, too.

So ask questions, test your ideas, and make lots of mistakes! Want inspiration? Grab a friend and take a trip to a science center or technology museum. They're just the kind of places to put curious, creative minds to work—and play.

Acknowledgments

A second book that answers kids' wacky and wonderful science questions? Yes, please! I'm over the moon that I again got to work with an amazing group of people to create *Why Does My Shadow Follow Me?* A massive thank you to all the Ontario Science Centre staff who were so creative and thorough with their answers and generous with their time: Rich, Mary Jane, Sean, Teressa, Raluca, Simon, Donna, Rocio, Rachel, Walter, Martin, Bhavleen, Jen, Oriana, Christine, Liona, and Zoe (thanks for the extra notes!). Kudos also go to Kevin Von Appen, expert project wrangler and timekeeper, who kept things moving forward at a speedy pace. No small feat. At Annick Press, an enormous shout-out to Claire Caldwell, whose calm, steady presence and red-pen brilliance made working with her a snap . . . again! Much gratitude to Kaela Cadieux, Paul Covello, Becky Noelle, Doeun Rivendell, and Wendy Thomas. Thanks a million to Dayle Petty, plus Sylvia Greening and Michael McLaughlin at Transcript Heroes, for the quick, precise interview transcriptions. And especially Suharu Ogawa, who is not only a top-notch illustrator but is now a dear friend. Finally, to all the kids who have questions about this vast, messy, glorious universe (that means you!), keep asking them. You never know—they could end up in a book.

—Kira Vermond

As the Ontario Science Centre team once again came together to talk, laugh, scratch our heads, and come up with answers to these fabulous questions, we were contemplating a changed world. The COVID-19 quarantine had us working from home, meeting on video, and seeing how science—with unprecedented focus, global collaboration, and speed—was showing humanity the way through a shared crisis.

Never has it been more important to fearlessly ask, test, and repeat. Never has it been more important for us to do that together. And never has it been more important for kids to connect their natural joy and skill in exploring their world with the process of science—and to trust that it works.

Teressa Black; Simon Chang; Mary Jane Conboy, PhD; Liona Davies; Raluca Ellis; Alicia Farrow; Martin Fischer; Zoe Fitzgerald; Donna Francis; Karen Hager; Julie Jones; Bhavleen Kaur; Vanessa Lu; Rocio Navarro; Jennifer O'Leary; Catherine Paisley; Christine Russell; Lorrie Ann Smith; Walter Stoddard; Oriana Vella-Zarb; Rich Vieira; Rachel Ward-Maxwell, PhD; Sean Lee Ying—thanks for answers that spark even more curiosity!

And special thanks again to Chris Caira, Lorraine Sit, and the rest of the Maker Bean Cafe staff at the Ontario Science Centre, who have continued to gather some pretty great questions while serving up some pretty great coffee.

—Kevin Von Appen
Director, Science Communication
Ontario Science Centre

HUGE thanks to the kids whose fascinating, thoughtful, creative, and sometimes just plain weird science questions made this book possible:

Adi, Adley, Ahmed, Alex, Anderson, Asahi, Avery, Benjamin, Bethany, Caitlin, Camdyn, Camer, Doevany, Elon, Emerson, Emily, Emma, Ezra, Fer, Gavin, Hannah, Jaiden, James, Jessey, Julie, Kignon, Logan, Lucas, Lyra, Lysandra, Maito, Mia, Mohamed, Morgan, Nehchal, Neil, Nico, Noor, Sabrina, Sam, Sammy, Simona, Sophia, Story, Teddy, Truman, Valenzia, William, Zayd, and Zipona.

Further Reading

Anderson, Amy, and Brian Anderson. *Space Dictionary for Kids: The Everything Guide for Kids Who Love Space*. Waco, TX: Prufrock Press, 2016

Brusatte, Steve. *The Rise and the Fall of the Dinosaurs: A New History of a Lost World*. New York: HarperCollins, 2018

Rosling, Hans, Anna Rosling Rönnlund, and Ola Rosling. *Factfulness: Ten Reasons We're Wrong About the World—and Why Things Are Better Than You Think*. New York: Flatiron Books, 2018

Verstraete, Larry, and Julius Csotonyi. *Dinosaurs of the Deep: Discover Prehistoric Marine Life*. Winnipeg: Turnstone Press, 2016

Watson, Galadriel, and Samantha Dixon. *Running Wild: Awesome Animals in Motion*. Toronto: Annick Press, 2020

Select Sources

Secondary sources consulted by Kira Vermond.

CHAPTER 1: CUTE CRITTERS AND UP-ROAR-IOUS CREATURES

Why do dogs see in black and white?

Peter Tyson, "Dogs' Dazzling Sense of Smell," NOVA Science Trust website, PBS, October 3, 2012,
https://www.pbs.org/wgbh/nova/article/dogs-sense-of-smell/

Why don't owls fly in the morning?

Murad Ali Khan, "What Do Owls Eat – Owls Diet," Kidz Feed,
https://kidzfeed.com/what-do-owls-eat/

Why do scorpions glow under ultraviolet light?

David Max Braun, "Scorpions That Glow in the Dark," National Geographic website, October 24, 2011,
https://blog.nationalgeographic.org/2011/10/24/scorpions-that-glow-in-the-dark/

Eliza Buzacott-Speer, "Why do scorpions glow in the dark? It could just be a fluke, scientists say," ABC Radio Brisbane website, October 25, 2017,
https://www.abc.net.au/news/2017-10-25/why-do-scorpions-glow-in-the-dark-queensland-museum/9076978

"Scorpions glow in the dark to detect moonlight," *New Scientist* website, December 8, 2010,
https://www.newscientist.com/article/mg20827903-700-scorpions-glow-in-the-dark-to-detect-moonlight/

Natalie Wolchover, "Glow-in-the-dark scorpions: Why do they do it?," NBC News.com, May 13, 2011,
http://www.nbcnews.com/id/43027595/ns/technology_and_science-science/t/glow-in-the-dark-scorpions-why-do-they-do-it/

Why don't wasps make honey?

Emily Osterloff, "What do wasps do?," Natural History Museum website,
https://www.nhm.ac.uk/discover/what-do-wasps-do.html

"What's the difference between bees, wasps and hornets?," BBC Newsround, August 29, 2018,
https://www.bbc.co.uk/newsround/45194754

Paul Brown, "Why climate change is good news for wasps," *The Guardian* website, February 6, 2017,
https://www.theguardian.com/environment/2017/feb/06/climate-change-good-news-wasps-weatherwatch

Why do bees sting?

"Why do bees sting?," The Children's Museum of Indianapolis website, May 19, 2016,
https://www.childrensmuseum.org/blog/why-do-bees-sting

Jim and Leona Meeks, "How Do Animals Protect Themselves?," Michigan Reach Out!,
http://www.reachoutmichigan.org/funexperiments/quick/animalprotect.html

What is the oldest animal on Earth?

Elahe Izadi, "A sea sponge the size of a minivan could be one of the world's oldest living animals," *The Washington Post* website, May 12, 2016,
https://www.washingtonpost.com/news/speaking-of-science/wp/2016/05/26/a-sea-sponge-the-size-of-a-minivan-could-be-one-of-the-worlds-oldest-living-animals/

Adam Millward, "Introducing Jonathan, the world's oldest animal on land at 187 years old," Guinness World Records website, February 27, 2019,
https://www.guinnessworldrecords.com/news/2019/2/introducing-jonathan-the-worlds-oldest-animal-on-land-561882/

Sara LaJeunesse, "Corals much older than previously thought, study finds," *Penn State News* website, November 30, 2016,
https://news.psu.edu/story/439785/2016/11/30/corals-much-older-previously-thought-study-finds

Why are sharks so scary?

Alina Bradford, "Facts About Whale Sharks," Live Science, July 14, 2016,
https://www.livescience.com/55412-whale-sharks.html

"Dwarf Lantern Shark," Smithsonian Ocean website,
https://ocean.si.edu/ocean-life/sharks-rays/dwarf-lantern-shark

Why didn't sharks become extinct with the dinosaurs?
John Pickrell, "Mass Shark Extinction Triggered by Dinosaur-Killing Asteroid," National Geographic website, August 2, 2018,
https://www.nationalgeographic.com/science/2018/08/news-shark-dinosaur-asteroid-extinction/

Lucy Jones, "The epic history of sharks," BBC Earth website, October 3, 2015,
http://www.bbc.com/earth/story/20151003-the-epic-history-of-sharks

Lucas Joel, "The secrets of how sharks survived so many of Earth's mass extinctions," *New Scientist* website, June 26, 2019,
https://www.newscientist.com/article/mg24232360-900-the-secrets-of-how-sharks-survived-so-many-of-earths-mass-extinctions/

How do scientists know a T-Rex was standing on two feet?
"Dinosaurs: Two legs or four?," *The Guardian* website, February 7, 2009,
https://www.theguardian.com/science/2009/feb/07/dinosaurs-evolution-bipeds-quadrupeds

Are birds really dinosaurs?
"Are Birds Really Dinosaurs?," Dinobuzz: Current Topics Concerning Dinosaurs, UC Museum of Paleontology Berkeley website, January 22, 1998,
https://ucmp.berkeley.edu/diapsids/avians.html

"The Dromaeosauridae," UC Museum of Paleontology Berkeley website, November 24, 1995,
https://ucmp.berkeley.edu/diapsids/saurischia/dromaeosauridae.html

Emily Singer, "How Dinosaurs Shrank and Became Birds," *Quanta Magazine*, syndicated on *Scientific American* website, June 12, 2015,
https://www.scientificamerican.com/article/how-dinosaurs-shrank-and-became-birds/

Lisa Hendry, "Why are birds the only surviving dinosaurs?," The Natural History Museum website,
https://www.nhm.ac.uk/discover/why-are-birds-the-only-surviving-dinosaurs.html

Riley Black, "What Happened in the Seconds, Hours, Weeks After the Dino-Killing Asteroid Hit Earth?," *Smithsonian Magazine* website, August 9, 2016,
https://www.smithsonianmag.com/science-nature/what-happened-seconds-hours-weeks-after-dino-killing-asteroid-hit-earth-180960032/

John Pickrell, "How Did Dino-Era Birds Survive the Asteroid 'Apocalypse'?," National Geographic website, May 24, 2018,
https://www.nationalgeographic.com/news/2018/05/dinosaurs-asteroid-birds-forests-fires-paleontology-science/

Hannah Waters, "How Birds Survived the Asteroid Impact That Wiped Out the Dinosaurs," National Audubon Society website, May 24, 2018,
https://www.audubon.org/news/how-birds-survived-asteroid-impact-wiped-out-dinosaurs

CHAPTER 2: THE WORLD INSIDE US

What makes us humans?
"What is Genetics?," The Gene Scene, American Museum of Natural History website,
https://www.amnh.org/explore/ology/genetics

"What Is a Gene?," reviewed by KidsHealth Medical Experts, KidsHealth from Nemours,
https://kidshealth.org/en/kids/what-is-gene.html

Melissa Hogenboom, "The traits that make human beings unique," BBC Future website, July 6, 2015,
https://www.bbc.com/future/article/20150706-the-small-list-of-things-that-make-humans-unique

Why do we have butts?
Heather Radke and Matt Kielty, "Man Against Horse," produced by Matt Kielty, Rachel Cusick, and Simon Adler, Radiolab, podcast audio, December 28, 2019,
https://www.wnycstudios.org/podcasts/radiolab/articles/man-against-horse

Dennis M. Bramble and Daniel E. Lieberman, "Endurance running and the evolution of *Homo*," *Nature* 432 (November 2004): 345–352
https://www.nature.com/articles/nature03052

Jack Scanlan, "Ask evolution: Why do we have butt cheeks?," SBS website, July 8, 2016,
https://www.sbs.com.au/topics/science/humans/article/2016/06/29/ask-evolution-why-we-have-butt-cheeks

Why do we grow hair?
Fiona MacDonald, "Why Do We Have Body Hair?," ScienceAlert, September 30, 2015,
https://www.sciencealert.com/watch-why-do-we-have-body-hair

Rachel Feltman and Sarah Kaplan, "Dear Science: Why does the hair on my head grow longer than the hair on my body?," *The Washington Post* website, July 19, 2016,
https://www.washingtonpost.com/news/speaking-of-science/wp/2016/07/19/dear-science-why-does-the-hair-on-my-head-grow-longer-than-the-hair-on-my-body/

How many times can you spin before you puke?
Julie Beck, "The Mysterious Science of Motion Sickness," *The Atlantic* website, February 17, 2015,
https://www.theatlantic.com/health/archive/2015/02/the-mysterious-science-of-motion-sickness/385469/

Miriam Kramer, "How Do You Puke Without Gravity?," Space.com, video, April 26, 2013,
https://www.space.com/20850-space-puke-astronaut-video.html

"Why does spinning make you feel sick?," The Naked Scientists, March 16, 2008,
https://www.thenakedscientists.com/articles/questions/why-does-spinning-make-you-feel-sick

Why does my pee smell?

"Your Urinary System," reviewed by KidsHealth Medical Experts, KidsHealth from Nemours, https://kidshealth.org/en/kids/pee.html

Rose Kivi, "What Causes Abnormal Urine Odor?," Healthline, medically reviewed by Carissa Stephens, RN, CCRN, CPN, July 29, 2019, https://www.healthline.com/health/urine-odor#asparagus

Joseph Stromberg, "Why Asparagus Makes Your Urine Smell," *Smithsonian Magazine* website, May 3, 2013, https://www.smithsonianmag.com/science-nature/why-asparagus-makes-your-urine-smell-49961252/

How does sound get to our brains?

"How Do We Hear?," National Institute on Deafness and Other Communication Disorders website, U.S. Department of Health and Human Services, updated January 3, 2018, https://www.nidcd.nih.gov/health/how-do-we-hear

Do we all see color the same?

Tim Jewell, "Tetrachromacy ('Super Vision')," Healthline, medically reviewed by Ann Marie Griff, OD, October 24, 2018, https://www.healthline.com/health/tetrachromacy#tests

"Do You See What I See?," Wonderopolis, http://www.wonderopolis.org/wonder/do-you-see-what-i-see

S. Deleniv, "The Mystery of Tetrachromacy: If 12% of Women Have Four Cone Types in Their Eyes, Why Do So Few of Them Actually See More Colours?," The Neurosphere, December 17, 2015, https://theneurosphere.com/2015/12/17/the-mystery-of-tetrachromacy-if-12-of-women-have-four-cone-types-in-their-eyes-why-do-so-few-of-them-actually-see-more-colours/

Why are games so fun?

Ryan, "Video games are fun. Here's why, and how they hook us.," iD Tech, November 22, 2019, https://www.idtech.com/blog/what-makes-video-games-fun

Kenneth R. Ginsburg, the Committee on Communications, and the Committee on Psychosocial Aspects of Child and Family Health, "The Importance of Play in Promoting Healthy Child Development and Maintaining Strong Parent-Child Bonds," *Pediatrics* 119 (January 2007): 182–191, https://pediatrics.aappublications.org/content/119/1/182

Tom Bawden, "Crocodiles just wanna have fun: Scientists observe deadly reptiles at play," *Independent* website, February 11, 2015, https://www.independent.co.uk/environment/crocodiles-just-wanna-have-fun-scientists-observe-deadly-reptiles-at-play-10039757.html

Will humans ever fly?

"What Is Aerodynamics?," NASA Knows! (Grades K-4 Series), NASA website, June 4, 2011, https://www.nasa.gov/audience/forstudents/k-4/stories/nasa-knows/what-is-aerodynamics-k4.html

Is genetic mutation that creates super abilities possible?

Adam Lee, "4 beneficial evolutionary mutations that humans are undergoing right now," Big Think, October 5, 2011, https://bigthink.com/daylight-atheism/evolution-is-still-happening-beneficial-mutations-in-humans

Lynn M. Boyden et al., "High Bone Density Due to a Mutation in LDL-Receptor–Related Protein 5," *The New England Journal of Medicine* 346 (2002): 1513–1521, https://www.nejm.org/doi/full/10.1056/NEJMoa013444#t=article

Lydia Ramsey, "8 Genetic Mutations That Can Give You 'Superpowers'," Business Insider, featured on ScienceAlert, May 31, 2017, https://www.sciencealert.com/8-genetic-mutations-that-can-give-you-superpowers

Lydia Ramsey, "A tiny percentage of the population needs only 4 hours of sleep per night," Business Insider website, November 11, 2015, https://www.businessinsider.com/people-who-sleep-short-hours-2015-11

"Mutations and Disease," The Tech Interactive, Stanford at the Tech, https://genetics.thetech.org/about-genetics/mutations-and-disease

Leslie A. Pray, "DNA Replication and Causes of Mutation," *Nature Education* 1, no. 1 (2008): 214, on Scitable by *Nature Education* website, https://www.nature.com/scitable/topicpage/dna-replication-and-causes-of-mutation-409/

CHAPTER 3: THIS PLANET WE CALL HOME

Why do we have to go outside?

Jamie Ducharme, "Spending Just 20 Minutes in a Park Makes You Happier. Here's What Else Being Outside Can Do for Your Health," *Time* website, February 28, 2019, https://time.com/5539942/green-space-health-wellness/

Shankar Vedantam, Thomas Lu, and Tara Boyle, "You 2.0: Our Better Nature," on Hidden Brain, NPR, podcast audio, August 12, 2019, https://www.npr.org/2019/08/12/750538458/you-2-0-our-better-nature

Simon Worrall, "We Are Wired To Be Outside," National Geographic website, February 12, 2017, https://www.nationalgeographic.com/news/2017/02/nature-fix-brain-happy-florence-williams/

How did water get on Earth?

"10 Interesting Things About Water," NASA Climate Kids, last updated April 23, 2020,
https://climatekids.nasa.gov/10-things-water/

"Planet Earth - a water world," ESA Kids, European Space Agency, last updated December 6, 2004,
https://www.esa.int/kids/en/learn/Our_Universe/Planets_and_moons/Planet_Earth_-_a_water_world

Brian Greene, "How Did Water Come to Earth?," *Smithsonian Magazine* website, May 2013,
https://www.smithsonianmag.com/science-nature/how-did-water-come-to-earth-72037248/

What makes volcanoes explode?

"The Big Question: Why do volcanoes erupt?," BBC Newsround, May 13, 2018,
https://www.bbc.co.uk/newsround/44100737

"Curious Kids: Why do volcanoes erupt?," posted by The Conversation, ABC Education, August 14, 2018,
https://education.abc.net.au/newsandarticles/blog/-/b/2936075/curious-kids-why-do-volcanoes-erupt

Ruth A. Musgrave, "Volcano," National Geographic Kids website,
https://kids.nationalgeographic.com/explore/science/volcano/

Kacey Deamer, "Magma Power: Scientists Drill into Volcano to Harness its Energy," Live Science, February 9, 2017,
https://www.livescience.com/57833-scientists-drill-volcano-core-geothermal-energy.html

Peter Tyson, "Can We Predict Eruptions?," NOVA Online, PBS, excerpted and updated from *Technology Review*, January 1996,
https://www.pbs.org/wgbh/nova/vesuvius/predict.html

Why are flowers different colors?

Austa Somvichian-Clausen, "Pictures Capture the Invisible Glow of Flowers," National Geographic website, February 23, 2018,
https://www.nationalgeographic.com/photography/proof/2018/february/glowing-flowers-ultraviolet-light/#/07-glowing-flowers-White-Leadtree-1.jpg

Sara Reverté, Javier Retana, José M. Gómez, and Jordi Bosch, "Pollinators show flower colour preferences but flowers with similar colours do not attract similar pollinators," *Annals of Botany* 118, no. 2 (August 2016): 249–257,
https://academic.oup.com/aob/article/118/2/249/1741474

"Fly Pollination," The U.S. Forest Service website, United States Department of Agriculture,
https://www.fs.fed.us/wildflowers/pollinators/animals/flies.shtml

How do mirrors reflect?

David Nield, "The Awesome Physics Behind How Mirrors Work," ScienceAlert, February 5, 2016,
https://www.sciencealert.com/how-do-mirrors-work

Anna Green, "How Do Mirrors Work?," Mental Floss, February 2, 2016,
https://www.mentalfloss.com/article/74633/how-do-mirrors-work

"The eyes," Sightsavers website,
https://www.sightsavers.org/protecting-sight/the-eyes/

What color is sunlight?

Dr. David P. Stern, "The Many Colors of Sunlight," NASA website, last updated September 23, 2004,
https://www-spof.gsfc.nasa.gov/stargaze/Sun4spec.htm

"What Color is the Sun?," Stanford Solar Center website,
http://solar-center.stanford.edu/SID/activities/GreenSun.html

How does static make hair fly?

"What Is Static Electricity?," Science Made Simple,
https://www.sciencemadesimple.com/static.html

"How Does Static Electricity Work?," Everyday Mysteries, Library of Congress website,
https://www.loc.gov/everyday-mysteries/item/how-does-static-electricity-work/

Science Buddies, "Attraction with Static Electricity," Bring Science Home, *Scientific American* website, January 12, 2012,
https://www.scientificamerican.com/article/bring-science-home-static-electricity-attraction/

How many people live on Earth?

"Current World Population," Worldometer,
https://www.worldometers.info/world-population/

Vivien Cumming, "How many people can our planet really support?," BBC Earth website, March 14, 2016,
http://www.bbc.com/earth/story/20160311-how-many-people-can-our-planet-really-support

"Hans Rosling's Important Truths about Population Growth and the Developing World," Farnam Street website,
https://fs.blog/2016/04/hans-rosling-population-growth/

CHAPTER 4: TREMENDOUS TECH AND INSPIRING INNOVATIONS

How do you get the strawberry in the strawberry candy?

C. Rose Kennedy, "The Flavor Rundown: Natural vs. Artificial Flavors," Science in the News (blog), the Graduate School of Arts and Sciences, Harvard University, September 21, 2015,
http://sitn.hms.harvard.edu/flash/2015/the-flavor-rundown-natural-vs-artificial-flavors/

"Where Do Flavors Come From?," Flavor & Extract Manufacturers Association website,
https://www.femaflavor.org/flavors-come

"Substances Added to Food (formerly EAFUS): 3-METHYL-3-PHENYL GLYCIDIC ACID ETHYL ESTER," U.S. Food and Drug Administration website, last updated May 8, 2020,
https://www.accessdata.fda.gov/scripts/fdcc/index.cfm?set=FoodSubstances&id=METHYLPHENYLGLYCIDICACIDETHYLESTER

Veronique Greenwood, "Sweet Memories: How Jelly Belly Invents Flavors," *The Atlantic* website, August 17, 2010,
https://www.theatlantic.com/health/archive/2010/08/sweet-memories-how-jelly-belly-invents-flavors/61477/

Why does my bag of popcorn explode after microwaving for two minutes?

"Why Does Popcorn Pop?," The Children's Museum of Indianapolis website, March 11, 2016,
https://www.childrensmuseum.org/blog/why-does-popcorn-pop

Why is glue sticky?

The Straight Dope Science Advisory Board, "How does glue work?," The Straight Dope website, August 1, 2006,
https://www.straightdope.com/columns/read/2257/how-does-glue-work/

Autumn Spanne, "Why Is Glue Sticky?," Mental Floss, April 30, 2018,
https://www.mentalfloss.com/article/76318/why-glue-sticky

When will they cure cancer?

Ethan Bilby, "Will we ever cure cancer?," *Horizon: The EU Research & Innovation Magazine* website, September 18, 2019,
https://horizon-magazine.eu/article/will-we-ever-cure-cancer.html

"Why haven't we cured cancer?," Worldwide Cancer Research website, September 16, 2019,
https://www.worldwidecancerresearch.org/stories/2019/september/why-havent-we-cured-cancer/

Bill Gates, "How we'll invent the future, by Bill Gates," *MIT Technology Review* website, February 27, 2019,
https://www.technologyreview.com/lists/technologies/2019/

Can stem cells bring back the dead?

"What is a stem cell?," yourgenome website, last updated August 17, 2017,
https://www.yourgenome.org/facts/what-is-a-stem-cell

Ted Ranosa, "Are We Close To Resurrecting The Dead? Scientists Revive Brain Cell Activities In Dead Pigs," *Tech Times* website, April 19, 2019,
https://www.techtimes.com/articles/241857/20190419/are-we-close-to-resurrecting-the-dead-scientists-revive-brain-cell-activities-in-dead-pigs.htm

Can we live forever one day?

"Canada: Life Expectancy," World Health Rankings,
https://www.worldlifeexpectancy.com/canada-life-expectancy

"North America - Life expectancy at birth," Index Mundi, last updated December 28, 2019,
https://www.indexmundi.com/facts/north-america/life-expectancy-at-birth

Karen Weintraub, "Aging Is Reversible—at Least in Human Cells and Live Mice," *Scientific American* website, December 15, 2016,
https://www.scientificamerican.com/article/aging-is-reversible-at-least-in-human-cells-and-live-mice/

Caleb E. Finch, "Evolution of the human lifespan and diseases of aging: Roles of infection, inflammation, and nutrition," *PNAS* 107 (January 26, 2010): 1718–1724,
https://www.pnas.org/content/107/suppl_1/1718

Why do we pollute?

Jasmine Malik Chua, "8 Inspiring Green Kids and Their Eco-Innovations," Inhabitat, August 4, 2010,
https://inhabitat.com/8-inspiring-green-kids-and-their-eco-innovations/max-wallack/

How does information travel so fast on the Internet?

Bernadette Johnson, "Can information travel faster than light?," HowStuffWorks.com, December 12, 2012,
https://electronics.howstuffworks.com/future-tech/information-travel-faster-than-light1.htm

Is there Wi-Fi in space?

"The Space Network: Cell Towers for Astronauts," NASA website,
https://www.nasa.gov/audience/foreducators/stem-on-station/downlinks-scan.html

Adrienne Lafrance, "The Internet in Space? Slow as Dial-Up," *The Atlantic* website, June 11, 2015,
https://www.theatlantic.com/technology/archive/2015/06/the-internet-in-space-slow-dial-up-lasers-satellites/395618/

CHAPTER 5: OUR OUT-OF-THIS-WORLD UNIVERSE

Why is there no gravity in space?

Bill Andrews, "20 Things You Didn't Know About Gravity," *Discover* Magazine website, July 18, 2013,
https://www.discovermagazine.com/the-sciences/20-things-you-didnt-know-about-gravity

When will the Sun explode?

Fraser Cain, "Will the Sun Explode?," Universe Today, January 6, 2014,
https://www.universetoday.com/107791/will-the-sun-explode/

What is the coldest star?

Jaime Lutz, "NASA Finds Coldest Star Ever, as Chilly as the Arctic," ABC News website, April 28, 2014,
https://abcnews.go.com/blogs/headlines/2014/04/nasa-finds-coldest-star-ever-as-chilly-as-the-arctic

Does bacteria grow in space?

Jennifer Yttri, PhD, "Bacteria: the Good, the Bad, and the Ugly," National Center for Health Research website,
http://www.center4research.org/bacteria-good-bad-ugly/

"NIH Human Microbiome Project defines normal bacterial makeup of the body," National Institutes of Health website, June 13, 2012,
https://www.nih.gov/news-events/news-releases/nih-human-microbiome-project-defines-normal-bacterial-makeup-body

Why are there astronauts in space when we have robots?

"Why do we send robots to space?," NASA Space Place, last updated September 14, 2020,
https://spaceplace.nasa.gov/space-robots/en/

How far is it possible to go in a spaceship?

Rachel Courtland, "Final Frontier: How Far Could Astronauts Go?," ABC News website, September 25, 2009,
https://abcnews.go.com/Technology/travel-spaceship/story?id=8674256

Elizabeth Howell, "Voyager 1: Earth's Farthest Spacecraft," Space.com, March 1, 2018,
https://www.space.com/17688-voyager-1.html

Voyager Mission Status, NASA Jet Propulsion Laboratory website,
https://voyager.jpl.nasa.gov/mission/status/

Ken Croswell, "How Far Can Voyager 1 Go?," *Smithsonian Magazine* website, April 2013,
https://www.smithsonianmag.com/science-nature/how-far-can-voyager-i-go-4728025/

How do people survive on Mars?

"Goal 4: Prepare for the Human Exploration of Mars," NASA: Mars Exploration website,
https://mars.nasa.gov/programmissions/science/goal4/

Karla Lant, "It's Official. Humans Are Going to Mars. NASA Has Unveiled Their Mission," Futurism website, April 28, 2017,
https://futurism.com/its-official-humans-are-going-to-mars-nasa-has-unveiled-their-mission

"Your Weight on Mars," Exploratorium, The Museum of Science, Arts, and Human Perception website,
https://www.exploratorium.edu/mars/yourweight.php

"Your Age on Mars," Exploratorium, The Museum of Science, Arts, and Human Perception website,
https://www.exploratorium.edu/mars/yourage.php

Index